Daily

MINDFULNESS

365 DAYS

*of Present, Calm,
Exquisite Living*

FAMILIUS

The brilliance of the rose and the whiteness of the lily do not lessen the perfume of the violet or the sweet simplicity of the daisy. I understood that if all the lowly flowers wished to be roses, nature would lose its springtide beauty, and the fields would no longer be enamelled with lovely hues.

—*Saint Thérèse of Lisieux*, The Story of a Soul

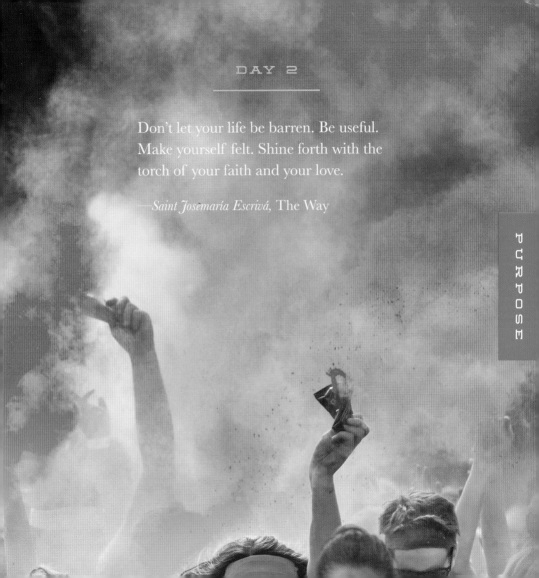

Don't let your life be barren. Be useful.
Make yourself felt. Shine forth with the
torch of your faith and your love.

—*Saint Josemaría Escrivá,* The Way

PURPOSE

PRESENCE

Do the things external which
fall upon thee distract thee?
Give thyself time to learn
something new and good, and
cease to be whirled around.
But then thou must also avoid
being carried about the other
way. For those too are triflers
who have wearied themselves
in life by their activity, and
yet have no object to which to
direct every movement, and,
in a word, all their thoughts.

—*Marcus Aurelius,*
Meditations, Book 2

Neither family, nor privilege, nor wealth, nor anything but Love can light that beacon which a man must steer by when he sets out to live the better life.

—*Plato*, Symposium

INTENTION

Happiness is a butterfly,
which when pursued, is
always beyond your grasp,
but which, if you will sit
down quietly, may alight
upon you.

—*Unknown*

CALM

DAY 6

Show me your hands. Do
they have scars from giving?
Show me your feet. Are they
wounded in service? Show
me your heart. Have you
left a place for divine love?

—*Archbishop Fulton J. Sheen*

DAY 7

The power of finding beauty
in the humblest things makes
home happy and life lovely.

—*Louisa May Alcott,* Jack and Jill:
A Village Story

Through the Thou a person becomes I.

—*Martin Buber,* I and Thou

PURPOSE

All that happens to us, including our humiliations, our misfortunes, our embarrassments, all is given to us as raw material, as clay, so that we may shape our art.

—*Jorge Luis Borges*

Contemplation is both the highest form of
activity (since the intellect is the highest thing
in us, and the objects that it apprehends are
the highest things that can be known), and
also it is the most continuous, because we are
more capable of continuous contemplation
than we are of any practical activity.

—*Aristotle*, Nicomachean Ethics

PRESENCE

DAY 11

No one should be discouraged
. . . who can make constant
progress, even though it be slow.

—*Plato*, Sophist

Time heals all wounds.

—*Terence,* Heauton Timorumenos

CALM

For each man loves himself,
not that he himself may get
from himself some reward for
his own affection, but because
each one is of himself dear to
himself. And unless this same
feeling shall be transferred to
Friendship, a true friend will
never be discovered. For [a true
friend] is, indeed, one who is,
as it were, a second self.

—*Cicero*, De Amicitia

CONNECTION

DAY 14

People from a planet without flowers would
think we must be mad with joy the whole time
to have such things about us.

—Iris Murdoch, A Fairly Honourable Defeat

GRATITUDE

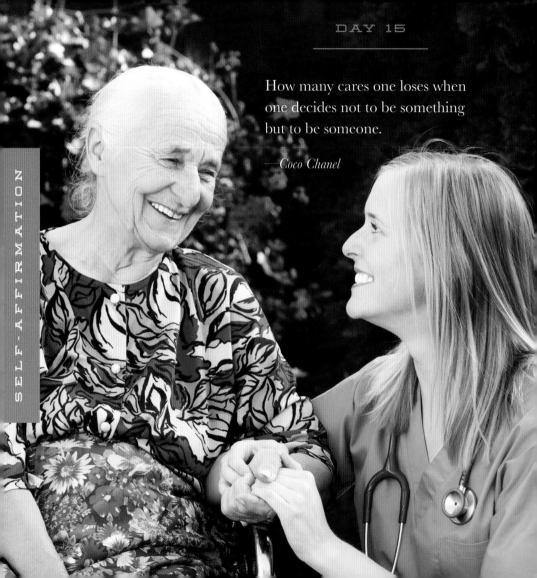

SELF-AFFIRMATION

How many cares one loses when one decides not to be something but to be someone.

—*Coco Chanel*

Come, seek, for search is the foundation of fortune:
every success depends upon focusing the heart.

—*Rumi*, Jewels of Remembrance

PURPOSE

Do not yield to misfortunes, but
advance more boldly to meet them,
as your fortune permits you.

—*Virgil*

PRESENCE

DAY 18

Living with intention
means saying no to the
things that aren't important
to us so we can say yes to
what matters most.

—*Crystal Paine*

Everything changes and nothing stands still. *Heraclitus*

CALM

DAY 20

The people we surround ourselves with either raise or lower our standards. They either help us to become the-best-version-of-ourselves or encourage us to become lesser versions of ourselves. We become like our friends. No man becomes great on his own. No woman becomes great on her own. The people around them help to make them great.

—*Matthew Kelly,* The Rhythm of Life

DAY 21

Every object and being in the universe is
a jar overflowing with wisdom and beauty,
a drop of the Tigris that cannot be contained
by any skin. Every jarful spills and makes the earth
more shining, as though covered in satin.

—*Rumi*

There is a vitality, a life force, an energy, a quickening that is translated through you into action, and because there is only one of you in all of time, this expression is unique. And if you block it, it will never exist through any other medium and it will be lost.

—*Martha Graham*

SELF-AFFIRMATION

DAY 23

You can't use up
creativity. The
more you use, the
more you have.

—*Maya Angelou*

DAY 24

One of the most important—and
most neglected—elements in the
beginnings of the interior life is
the ability to respond to reality,
to see the value and the beauty in
ordinary things, to come alive to the
splendor that is all around us . . .

—*Thomas Merton,* No Man Is an Island

INTENTION

A field, though fertile, cannot yield a
harvest without cultivation.

—*Cicero*, Tusculan Disputations

If you are irritated by
every rub,

how will your mirror be
polished?

—*Rumi*

Love is not affectionate feeling,
but a steady wish for the loved
person's ultimate good as far
as it can be obtained.

—*C. S. Lewis*

CONNECTION

The next time you look into
the mirror, just look at the
way the ears rest next to the
head; look at the way the
hairline grows; think of all the
little bones in your wrist. It is
a miracle.

—*Martha Graham*

GRATITUDE

DAY 29

Always be a first-
rate version of
yourself instead of a
second-rate version
of somebody else.

—*Judy Garland*

Never place a period
where God has
placed a comma.

—*Gracie Allen*

PURPOSE

DAY 31

I think, therefore I am.

—*Descartes*

Only the wise are grateful
for a remonstrance. Ever the
wise profit by the opportunity
to become wiser yet; ever the
godly are the best learners.

—*Proverbs 9:8–9*

INTENTION

DAY 33

Oh, God of Dust and Rainbows,
Help us to see
That without the dust the rainbow
Would not be.

—*Langston Hughes*

CALM

True love, in fact, is not an outward act; it is not giving something in a paternalistic way in order to assuage the conscience, but to accept those who are in need of our time, our friendship, our help. It means living to serve, overcoming the temptation to satisfy ourselves.

—*Pope Francis*

CONNECTION

DAY 35

Pleasure is very seldom found where it is
sought. Our brightest blazes of gladness are
commonly kindled by unexpected sparks. The
flowers which scatter their odours from time
to time in the paths of life grow up without
culture from seeds scattered by chance.

—*Samuel Johnson*

DAY 36

The best colour in the
whole world is the one
that looks good on you.

—Coco Chanel

PURPOSE

DAY 37

Dreaming, after all,
is a form of planning.

—*Gloria Steinem*

Enjoy the journey. Enjoy the journey, and the hard work and the sacrifices and opportunities it takes to get somewhere, because it will all make you better at what you do when you arrive.

—*Tabitha D'umo*

PRESENCE

INTENTION

DAY 39

Practice means to perform, in
the face of all obstacles, some
act of vision, of faith, of desire.
Practice is a means of inviting the
perfection desired.

—*Martha Graham*

CALM

DAY 40

If you are wholly perplexed and in
straits, have patience, for patience
is the key to joy.

—*Rumi*

Friendship is unnecessary, like philosophy, like art . . . . It has no survival value; rather it is one of those things which give value to survival.

—*C. S. Lewis*, The Four Loves

CONNECTION

I would maintain
that thanks are the
highest form of
thought; and that
gratitude is happiness
doubled by wonder.

—*G. K. Chesterton*,
A Short History of
England

GRATITUDE

DAY 43

I used to have a certain dislike of the audience, not as individual people, but as a giant body who was judging me. Of course, it wasn't really them judging me. It was me judging me. Once I got past that fear, it freed me up, not just when I was performing but in other parts of my life.

—*Julie Andrews*

Nothing will ever be attempted
if all possible objections must
be first overcome.

—*Samuel Johnson,* Rasselas

PURPOSE

DAY 45

Life forms illogical
patterns. It is haphazard
and full of beauties which
I try to catch as they fly by,
for who knows whether any
of them will ever return?

—*Margot Fonteyn*

We suffer
primarily not from
our vices or our
weaknesses, but
from our illusions.

—*Daniel J. Boorstin*

INTENTION

DAY 47

There's only one great evil in
the world today. Despair.

—*Evelyn Waugh*

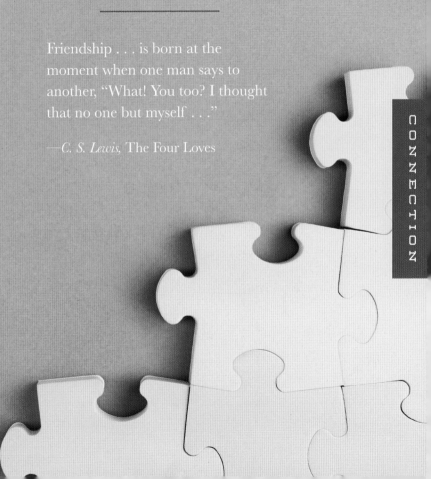

Friendship . . . is born at the moment when one man says to another, "What! You too? I thought that no one but myself . . ."

—*C. S. Lewis,* The Four Loves

CONNECTION

DAY 49

As we express our gratitude, we
must never forget that the highest
appreciation is not to utter words
but to live by them.

—*John F. Kennedy*

Be yourself by growing above yourself.
Don't stand in your own way. Let
us change with, and not against,
movement.

—*Jean Tinguely*

SELF-AFFIRMATION

DAY 51

Success is walking from
failure to failure with no
loss of enthusiasm.

—*Unknown*

My inspiration has been drawn from trees, from waves, from clouds, from the sympathies that exist between passion and the storm, between gentleness and the soft breeze, and the like, and I always endeavor to put into my movements a little of that divine continuity which gives to the whole of nature its beauty and its life.

—*Isadora Duncan*

PRESENCE

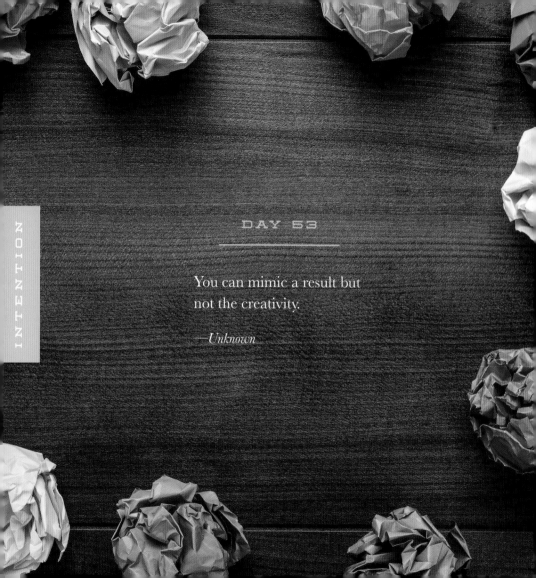

DAY 53

You can mimic a result but
not the creativity.

—*Unknown*

DAY 54

I try to avoid looking
forward or backward and
try to keep looking upward.

—*Charlotte Brontë*

CONNECTION

Love all, trust a few, do
wrong to none.

—*William Shakespeare,* All's
Well That Ends Well

Reflect upon your present
blessings, of which every
man has plenty; not on
your past misfortunes, of
which all men have some.

—*Charles Dickens*

GRATITUDE

Beauty is only skin deep. I think what's really important is finding a balance of mind, body, and spirit.

—*Jennifer Lopez*

SELF-AFFIRMATION

What is important is to believe
in something so strongly that
you're never discouraged.

—*Salma Hayek*

PURPOSE

Time is the substance I am made of. Time is a
river which sweeps me along, but I am the river; it
is a tiger which destroys me, but I am the tiger; it
is a fire which consumes me, but I am the fire.

—*Jorge Luis Borges*, Other Inquisitions

PRESENCE

DAY 60

It's not the load that breaks you down; it's the way you carry it.

—*Lou Holtz*

INTENTION

DAY 61

There are far, far better things
ahead than any we leave behind.

—*C. S. Lewis*

The best and greatest
winning is a true friend;
and the greatest loss is
the loss of time.

—*Pythagoras*

CONNECTION

GRATITUDE

Gratitude turns what we have into enough, and more. It turns denial into acceptance, chaos into order, confusion into clarity . . . [it] makes sense of our past, brings peace for today, and creates a vision for tomorrow.

—*Melody Beattie*

DAY 64

It takes a lot of courage
to face up to things you
can't do because we
feed ourselves so much
denial.

—*Zoe Saldana*

PURPOSE

The mystery of human existence lies not in just staying alive, but in finding something to live for.

—*Fyodor Dostoyevsky,*
The Brothers Karamazov

DAY 66

Only if we are secure in
our beliefs can we see the
comical side of the universe.

—*Flannery O'Connor*,
Mystery and Manners

DAY 67

We are what we pretend to
be, so we must be careful
about what we pretend to be.

—*Kurt Vonnegut*

DAY 68

Do what you can, with what you have,
where you are. —*Teddy Roosevelt*

DAY 69

If we would build on a sure
foundation in friendship, we
must love our friends for their
sakes rather than for our own.

—*Charlotte Brontë*

DAY 70

The world has enough beautiful mountains and meadows,
spectacular skies, and serene lakes. It has enough lush forests,
flowered fields, and sandy beaches. It has plenty of stars and the
promise of a new sunrise and sunset every day. What the world
needs more of is people to appreciate and enjoy it.

—*Michael Josephson*

DAY 71

Your self-worth is determined by
you. You don't have to depend on
someone telling you who you are.

—*Beyoncé*

PURPOSE

DAY 72

I have discovered in life that there are ways of getting
almost anywhere you want to go, if you really want to go.

—*Langston Hughes*

DAY 73

It is only with the heart that one can see
rightly; what is essential is invisible to the eye.

—*Antoine de Saint-Exupéry,* The Little Prince

Don't move the way fear
makes you move. Move
the way love makes you
move. Move the way joy
makes you move.

—*Osho*

INTENTION

You are the sky. Everything else—it's just the weather.

—*Pema Chödrön*

CALM

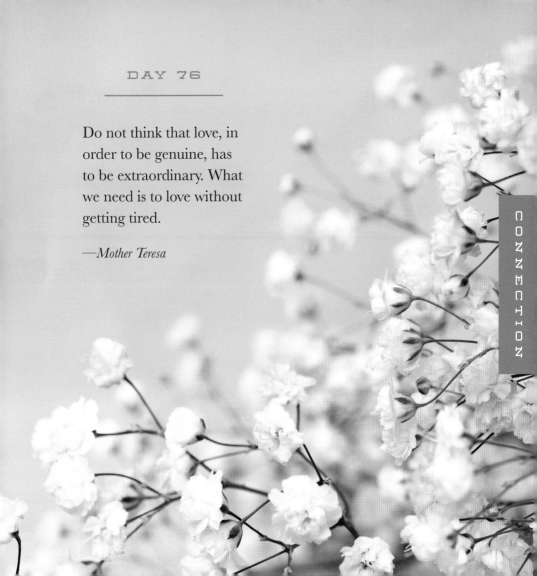

Do not think that love, in order to be genuine, has to be extraordinary. What we need is to love without getting tired.

—*Mother Teresa*

CONNECTION

The way to develop the best that is in a man is by appreciation and encouragement.

—*Charles Schwab*

GRATITUDE

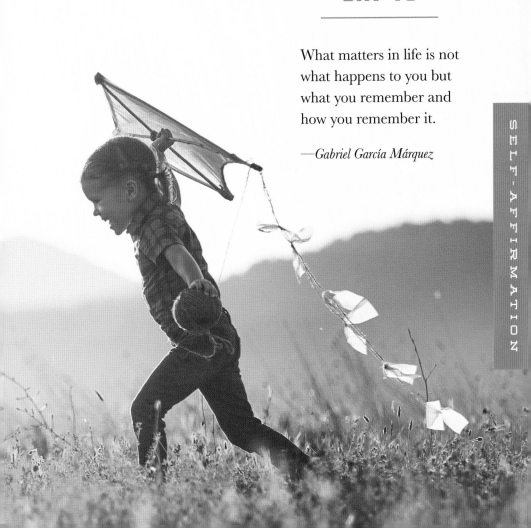

What matters in life is not
what happens to you but
what you remember and
how you remember it.

—*Gabriel García Márquez*

SELF-AFFIRMATION

If you look for truth, you may find comfort in the end; if you look for comfort, you will not get either comfort or truth—only soft soap and wishful thinking to begin, and in the end, despair.

—C. S. Lewis

PURPOSE

DAY 80

Wheresoever you go,
go with all your heart.

—*Confucius*

Look closely at the present
you are constructing: it
should look like the future
you are dreaming.

—*Alice Walker*

INTENTION

I have learned over the years
that when one's mind is
made up, this diminishes fear.

—*Rosa Parks*

CALM

DAY 83

If you can't feed a hundred
people, then feed just one.

—*Mother Teresa*

Gratitude is a currency that we can mint for ourselves, and spend without fear of bankruptcy.

—*Fred DeWitt Van Amburgh*

GRATITUDE

If all the world hated you, and believed you wicked, while your own conscience approved of you, and absolved you from guilt, you would not be without friends.

—*Charlotte Brontë*, Jane Eyre

The greatest challenge of the day is: how to bring about a revolution of the heart, a revolution which has to start with each one of us?

—*Dorothy Day*

PURPOSE

The noblest pleasure is
the joy of understanding.

—*Leonardo da Vinci*

It matters not what someone is born, but what they grow to be.

—*J. K. Rowling*, Harry Potter and the Goblet of Fire

INTENTION

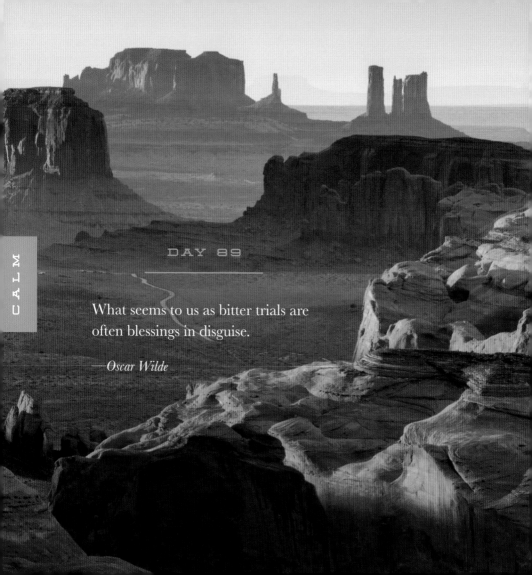

CALM

DAY 89

What seems to us as bitter trials are often blessings in disguise.

—*Oscar Wilde*

DAY 90

They do not love that
do not show their love.

—*William Shakespeare*, Two
Gentlemen of Verona

GRATITUDE

Let us rise up and be thankful, for if we
didn't learn a lot today, at least we learned
a little, and if we didn't learn a little, at least
we didn't get sick, and if we got sick, at least
we didn't die; so, let us all be thankful.

—*Unknown*

When I'm not feeling my best, I ask myself, "What are you gonna do about it?" I use the negativity to fuel the transformation into a better me.

—*Beyoncé*

SELF-AFFIRMATION

All the performances of human art, at which we look with praise or wonder, are instances of the resistless force of perseverance; it is by this that the quarry becomes a pyramid, and that distant countries are united with canals.

—*Samuel Johnson*

PURPOSE

The more clearly you understand yourself and your emotions, the more you become a lover of what is.

—*Baruch Spinoza*

PRESENCE

The task of the modern
educator is not to cut down
jungles but to irrigate deserts.

—*C. S. Lewis*

INTENTION

The ideal of calm exists in a sitting cat.

—*Jules Renard*

CALM

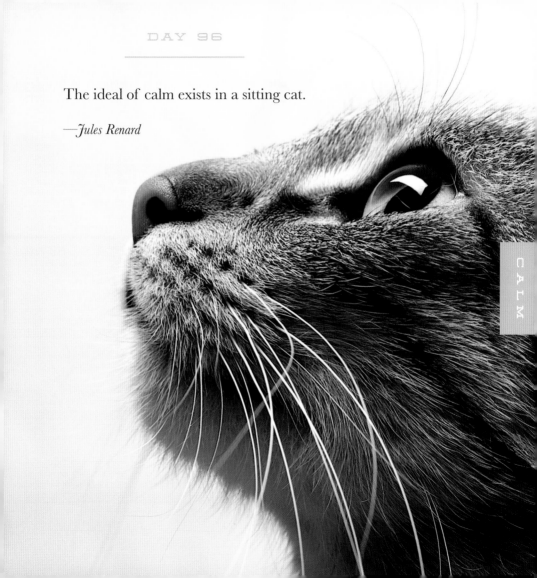

DAY 97

It is not the magnitude of our
actions but the amount of love
that is put into them that matters.

—*Mother Teresa*

DAY 98

Gratitude . . . opens
your eyes to the
limitless potential of
the universe, while
dissatisfaction closes
your eyes to it.

—*Stephen Richards*

GRATITUDE

DAY 99

They are able who
think they are able.

—*Virgil*

Don't worry about being effective. Just
concentrate on being faithful to the truth.

—*Dorothy Day*

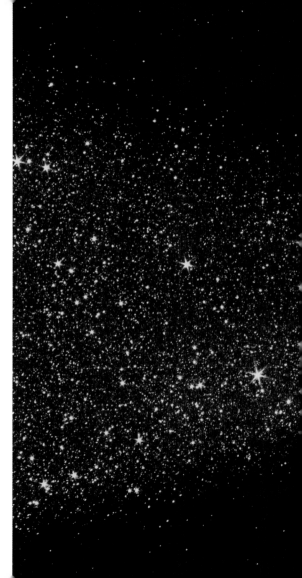

DAY 101

Nothing can be
loved or hated
unless it is first
understood.

—*Leonardo da Vinci*

We do not need magic to transform our world. We carry all the power we need inside ourselves already.

—*J. K. Rowling*

INTENTION

DAY 103

Maybe if we just lay beneath the stars
long enough, all our worries will dissipate
into the cosmos. And we can lay there
motionless, yet sailing across the stars.

—*Trevor Driggers*

CONNECTION

DAY 104

No friendship
is an accident.

—*O. Henry*

This is a wonderful day. I've never seen this one before.

—*Maya Angelou*

GRATITUDE

DAY 106

Be yourself; everyone
else is already taken.

—*Oscar Wilde*

SELF-AFFIRMATION

PURPOSE

DAY 107

The question isn't who is going to
let me; it's who is going to stop me.

—*Ayn Rand*

There are no uninteresting
things—only uninterested
people.

—*G. K. Chesterton*

PRESENCE

DAY 109

We cannot live better
than in seeking to
become better.

—*Socrates*

DAY 110

You cannot find peace by avoiding life.

—*Michael Cunningham,* The Hours

CALM

DAY 111

Kind words can be short and easy to speak, but their echoes are truly endless.

—*Mother Teresa*

DAY 112

Let us be grateful to
the people who make
us happy; they are the
charming gardeners who
make our souls blossom.

—*Marcel Proust*

GRATITUDE

DAY 113

No matter what, nobody can take away the dances you've already had.

—*Gabriel García Márquez*

DAY 114

What would you do if
you weren't afraid?

—*Sheryl Sandberg,* Lean In

All that is gold does not glitter,
Not all those who wander are lost.

—*J. R. R. Tolkien*, The Fellowship of
the Ring

PRESENCE

DAY 116

Keep true. Never be
ashamed of doing right.
Decide what you think
is right and stick to it.

—*George Eliot*

INTENTION

Peace cannot be kept by force; it can only be achieved by understanding.

—*Albert Einstein*

CALM

Friendship is something
in the soul. It is a thing
one feels. It is not a
return for something.

—*Graham Greene*

CONNECTION

DAY 119

Walk as if you are
kissing the earth with
your feet.

—*Thich Nhat Hanh*, Peace
Is Every Step

Nothing is ugly as long as it is alive.

—*Coco Chanel*

SELF-AFFIRMATION

PURPOSE

I am always doing that which I cannot do in order that I may learn how to do it.

—*Unknown*

An adventure is only an inconvenience rightly considered. An inconvenience is only an adventure wrongly considered.

—*G. K. Chesterton*

PRESENCE

INTENTION

The test of an adventure
is that when you're in the
middle of it, you say to
yourself, "Oh, now I've
got myself into an awful
mess; I wish I were sitting
quietly at home." And
the sign that something's
wrong with you is when
you sit quietly at home
wishing you were out
having lots of adventure.

—*Thornton Wilder*

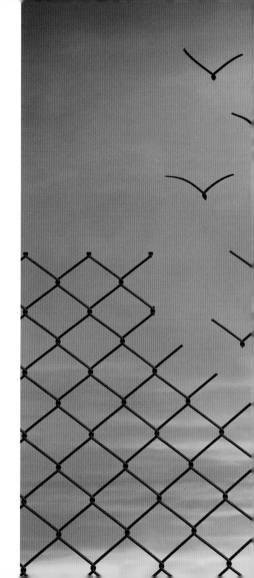

Letting go gives us freedom, and freedom
is the only condition for happiness. If, in
our heart, we still cling to anything—anger,
anxiety, or possessions—we cannot be free.

—*Thich Nhat Hanh*

CALM

CONNECTION

DAY 125

Love is a fruit in season at all times, and within reach of every hand. —*Mother Teresa*

DAY 126

Cultivate the habit of being
grateful for every good thing that
comes to you, and to give thanks
continuously. And because all
things have contributed to your
advancement, you should include
all things in your gratitude.

—*Ralph Waldo Emerson*

DAY 127

There is only one of you in
the world, just one, and if that
is not fulfilled, then something
has been lost.

—*Martha Graham*

Try not to become a
person of success but
rather a person of value.

—Albert Einstein

Hope is the gateway to
contemplation, because
contemplation is an
experience of divine
things and we cannot
experience what we do
not in some way possess.

—*Thomas Merton,* No Man
Is an Island

DAY 130

It will never rain roses: when
we want to have more roses, we
must plant more roses.

—*George Eliot*

CALM

Peace is always beautiful.

—*Walt Whitman, "The Sleepers"*

DAY 132

No matter what
happens in life, be good
to people. Being good
to people is a wonderful
legacy to leave behind.

—*Taylor Swift*

CONNECTION

GRATITUDE

In the end, maybe it's wiser to surrender before the miraculous scope of human generosity and to just keep saying thank you, forever and sincerely, for as long as we have voices.

—*Elizabeth Gilbert,* Eat, Pray, Love

DAY 134

Above all things, respect yourself.

—*Pythagoras*, Golden Verses

DAY 135

Cowards die many times
before their deaths.
The valiant never taste of
death but once.

—*William Shakespeare,*
Julius Caesar

The future starts
today, not tomorrow.

—*Pope John Paul II*

PRESENCE

If you would hit the mark, you must aim a little above it; Every arrow that flies feels the attraction of earth.

—*Henry Wadsworth Longfellow*, In the Harbor

INTENTION

A quiet conscience makes one strong!

—*Anne Frank*

CALM

CONNECTION

Old friends pass away; new friends
appear. It is just like the days.
An old day passes; a new day
arrives. The important thing is to
make it meaningful: a meaningful
friend—or a meaningful day.

—*Dalai Lama XIV*

If the only prayer you ever said was
thank you, that would be enough.

—*Meister Eckhart*

GRATITUDE

DAY 141

A bird sitting on a tree is never afraid
of the branch breaking, because her
trust is not on the branch but on her
own wings. Always believe in yourself.

—*Unknown*

Have the courage to follow
your heart and intuition. They
somehow already know what
you truly want to become.

—*Steve Jobs*

PURPOSE

There is geometry in the humming of the strings; there is music in the spacing of the spheres.

—*Pythagoras*

The man who moves a mountain begins by carrying away small stones.

—*Confucius*

INTENTION

CALM

DAY 145

It is not enough to win a war; it is
more important to organize the peace.

—*Aristotle*

Spread love everywhere you go.
Let no one ever come to you
without leaving happier.

—*Mother Teresa*

CONNECTION

DAY 147

Some people grumble that roses have thorns; I am grateful that thorns have roses.

—*Alphonse Karr,* A Tour Round My Garden

I feel my most beautiful when I am truly myself. Meaning, when I accept exactly where I am in time and space, and I'm not judging myself in any way, and I feel that I have the peace that comes with loving yourself and all of your flaws. I see so much now how beauty really does, as cliché as it sounds, emanate from within.

—*Gwyneth Paltrow*

SELF-AFFIRMATION

Taking initiative pays off. It is hard to visualize someone as a leader if she is always waiting to be told what to do.

—*Sheryl Sandberg,* Lean In

PURPOSE

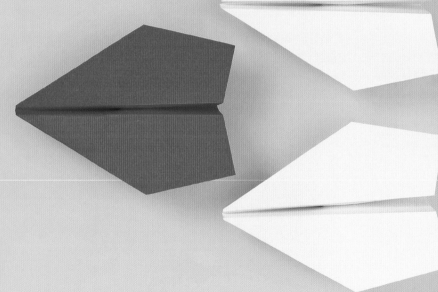

DAY 150

To ask the proper
question is half
of knowing.

—*Roger Bacon*

The real voyage of discovery consists not in seeking new landscapes, but in having new eyes.

—*Marcel Proust*

INTENTION

DAY 152

_____

If you cannot find peace within yourself,
you will never find it anywhere else.

—*Marvin Gaye*

C A L M

One can't love humanity. One can only love people.

—*Graham Greene*

CONNECTION

Appreciation is a wonderful
thing. It makes what is excellent
in others belong to us as well.

—*Voltaire*

GRATITUDE

DAY 155

I restore myself when I'm
alone. A career is born in
public—talent in privacy.

—*Marilyn Monroe*

I have not failed. I've just
found 10,000 ways that
won't work.

—*Thomas Edison*

We ought to be alive enough to reality to see beauty all around us. Beauty is simply reality itself, perceived in a special way that gives it a resplendent value of its own.

—*Thomas Merton*, No Man Is an Island

PRESENCE

INTENTION

DAY 158

Do not be afraid. Do not be satisfied
with mediocrity. Put out into the deep
and let down your nets for a catch.

—*Pope John Paul II*

DAY 159

Everywhere I have sought
peace and not found it, except
in a corner with a book.

—*Thomas à Kempis*

We ought so to behave to one another as to avoid making enemies of our friends, and at the same time to make friends of our enemies.

—*Pythagoras*

CONNECTION

And when you crush an apple with your teeth,
say to it in your heart:

Your seeds shall live in my body,
And the buds of your tomorrow shall blossom in my heart,
And your fragrance shall be my breath,
And together we shall rejoice through all the seasons.

—*Kahlil Gibran*

GRATITUDE

One of the best guides to how to be self-loving is to give ourselves the love we are often dreaming about receiving from others.

—*bell hooks*

SELF-AFFIRMATION

Success is often achieved
by those who don't know
that failure is inevitable.

—*Coco Chanel*

PURPOSE

Learn to breathe,
learn to speak, but
first . . . learn to feel.

—*Joan Crawford*

PRESENCE

Labor to keep alive in your breast
that little spark of celestial fire,
called conscience.

—*George Washington, "Rules of Civility"*

INTENTION

Instead of hating the people you think are war-makers, hate the appetites and disorder in your own soul, which are the causes of war. If you love peace, then hate injustice, hate tyranny, hate greed— but hate these things in yourself, not in another.

—*Thomas Merton*

CALM

CONNECTION

It's the friends you
can call up at 4 a.m.
that matter.

—*Marlene Dietrich*

Be thankful for your allotment in
an imperfect world. Though better
circumstances can be imagined, far
worse are nearer misses than you
probably care to realize.

—*Richelle E. Goodrich*

GRATITUDE

DAY 169

The whole point of being alive is to evolve into the complete person you were intended to be. —*Oprah Winfrey*

We know what we are, but
not what we may be.

—*William Shakespeare*, Hamlet

PURPOSE

Minor things can become moments of great revelation when encountered for the very first time.

—*Margot Fonteyn*

PRESENCE

DAY 172

I attribute my success
to this: I never gave
or took any excuse.

—*Florence Nightingale*

DAY 173

There is peace even in the storm.

—*Vincent van Gogh*

When you love someone, you love
the person as they are, and not as
you'd like them to be. —*Leo Tolstoy*

CONNECTION

Love casts out fear, and gratitude can conquer pride.

—*Louisa May Alcott,* Little Women

Being confident and believing in your own self-worth is necessary to achieving your potential.

—*Sheryl Sandberg*

SELF-AFFIRMATION

PURPOSE

DAY 177

I find that the harder I work,
the more luck I seem to have.

—*Thomas Jefferson*

To gain freedom is to gain simplicity.

—*Joan Miro*

PRESENCE

DAY 179

I plead with you—never, ever give up on
hope, never doubt, never tire, and never
become discouraged. Be not afraid.

—*Pope John Paul II*

Nothing can bring you peace but yourself.

—Ralph Waldo Emerson, "Self-Reliance"

CALM

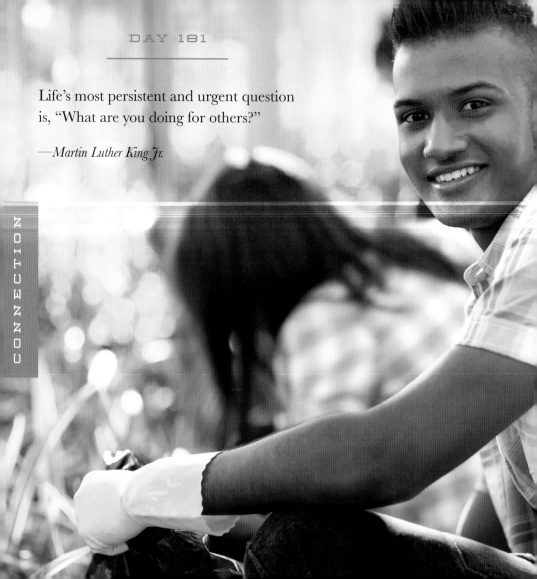

Life's most persistent and urgent question is, "What are you doing for others?"

—*Martin Luther King Jr.*

CONNECTION

DAY 182

Piglet noticed that even though
he had a Very Small Heart,
it could hold a rather large
amount of Gratitude.

—*A. A. Milne*, Winnie-the-Pooh

Everything, everything
shares life and has its
importance! Even the
most worn down of chair
carries inside the initial
force of the sap climbing
from the earth, out there
in the forest, and will still
be useful the day when,
broken into kindling, it
burns in some fireplace.

—*Antoni Tàpies*

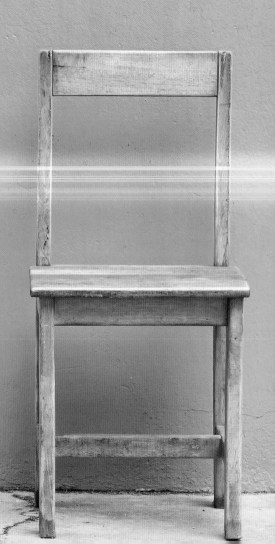

DAY 184

Only put off until tomorrow
what you are willing to die
having left undone.

—*Pablo Picasso*

DAY 185

It does not do to dwell on
dreams and forget to live.

—*J. K. Rowling*, Harry Potter
and the Sorcerer's Stone

DAY 186

Always try to keep a patch
of sky above your life.

—*Marcel Proust*, Swann's Way

DAY 187

I like trains. I like their rhythm,
and I like the freedom of being
suspended between two places,
all anxieties of purpose taken
care of: for this moment I
know where I am going.

—*Anna Funder,* Stasiland

DAY 188

Be kind, for everyone you
meet is fighting a hard battle.

—*Ian MacLaren*

Have no mean hours, but be grateful for
every hour, and accept what it brings.
The reality will make any sincere
record respectable. No day will have
been wholly misspent, if one sincere,
thoughtful page has been written.

—*Henry David Thoreau*, Journal

GRATITUDE

I figured that if I said it enough,
I would convince the world that
I really was the greatest.

—*Muhammad Ali*

SELF-AFFIRMATION

PURPOSE

People often say that
motivation doesn't last. Well,
neither does bathing—that's
why we recommend it daily.

—*Zig Ziglar*

Choose always the way that seems the best,
however rough it may be; custom will soon
render it easy and agreeable.

—*Pythagoras*

PRESENCE

The most difficult thing is the decision to act;
the rest is merely tenacity. —*Amelia Earhart*

INTENTION

Many a calm river begins as a turbulent waterfall,
yet none hurtles and foams all the way to the sea.

—*Mikhail Lermontov, A Hero of Our Time*

CALM

Love and compassion are
necessities, not luxuries. Without
them, humanity cannot survive.

—*Dalai Lama XIV*

CONNECTION

DAY 196

Always remember to
smile and look up at
what you got in life.

—*Marilyn Monroe*

DAY 197

Man is what he believes.

—*Anton Chekhov*

DAY 198

Life isn't about finding yourself.
Life is about creating yourself.

—Unknown

If your desires are not great, a little will seem much to you; for small appetite makes poverty equivalent to wealth.

—*Democritus*

PRESENCE

Twenty years from now you will be more disappointed by the things that you didn't do than by the ones you did do, so throw off the bowlines, sail away from safe harbor, catch the trade winds in your sails. Explore. Dream. Discover.

—*Unknown*

INTENTION

Life is what happens to you while
you're busy making other plans.

—*Unknown*

CALM

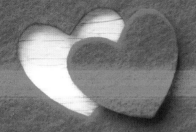

DAY 202

A person's rightful due is to
be treated as an object of
love, not as an object for use.

—*Pope John Paul II*

It has been said that life has treated
me harshly; and sometimes I have
complained in my heart because
many pleasures of human experience
have been withheld from me . . . if
much has been denied me, much,
very much, has been given me . . .

—*Helen Keller,* The Open Door

It's not the size
of the dog in the
fight; it's the size of
the fight in the dog.

—*Mark Twain*

SELF-AFFIRMATION

I find that when you have
a real interest in life and a
curious life, that sleep is not
the most important thing.

—*Martha Stewart*

PURPOSE

Wisely and slow.
They stumble that run fast.

—*William Shakespeare*, Romeo and Juliet

PRESENCE

DAY 207

The best time to plant a tree was twenty years ago. The second best time is now.

—*Chinese proverb*

DAY 208

Maturity, one discovers, has everything to do with the acceptance of "not knowing."

—*Mark Z. Danielewski,*
House of Leaves

CALM

DAY 209

The best way to
find out if you can
trust somebody is
to trust them.

—*Ernest Hemingway*

DAY 210

Rest and be thankful.

—*William Wordsworth*

Do not call the tortoise unworthy
because she is not something else.

—*Walt Whitman, "Song of Myself"*

SELF-AFFIRMATION

PURPOSE

DAY 212

There is some good
in this world, and it's
worth fighting for.

—*J. R. R. Tolkien*, The
Two Towers

A weed is but an unloved flower.

—*Ella Wheeler Wilcox, "The Weed"*

We don't receive wisdom; we must discover it for ourselves after a journey that no one can take for us or spare us.

—*Marcel Proust*

INTENTION

CALM

DAY 215

A man of calm is like a shady tree.
People who need shelter come to it.

—*Toba Beta*

Don't let us forget that the causes of human actions are usually immeasurably more complex and varied than our subsequent explanations of them.

—*Fyodor Dostoyevsky*, The Idiot

DAY 217

Let us learn to appreciate there will be times
when the trees will be bare and look forward
to the time when we may pick the fruit.

—*Anton Chekhov*

If a man does not
keep pace with his
companions, perhaps
it is because he hears a
different drummer. Let
him step to the music
which he hears, however
measured or far away.

—*Henry David Thoreau*,
Walden

SELF-AFFIRMATION

DAY 219

A goal is not always
meant to be reached; it
often serves simply as
something to aim at.

— *Bruce Lee*

When one door of
happiness closes,
another opens; but
often we look so
long at the closed
door that we do
not see the one
which has been
opened for us.

—*Helen Keller*

PRESENCE

DAY 221

Happiness is not
something ready
made. It comes from
your own actions.

—*Dalai Lama XIV*

I guess if you're ever going to feel
close to God it'll be while you're
looking at the heavens.

—*John Marsden,* The Night Is for Hunting

CALM

DAY 223

Nothing is menial
where there is love.

—*Pearl S. Buck*

DAY 224

When I started counting
my blessings, my whole
life turned around.

—*Willie Nelson*,
The Tao of Willie

I exist as I am; that is enough,
If no other in the world be aware I sit content,
And if each and all be aware I sit content.

—*Walt Whitman, "Song of Myself"*

SELF-AFFIRMATION

It is better to fail in originality than to succeed in imitation.

—*Herman Melville, "Hawthorne and His Mosses"*

PURPOSE

There was another life that I
might have had, but I am having
this one.

—*Kazuo Ishiguro*

PRESENCE

Life loves to be taken by the lapel and
told: "I'm with you, kid. Let's go."

—*Maya Angelou*

INTENTION

For all evils there are two remedies—time and silence.

—*Alexandre Dumas*, The Count of Monte Cristo

CALM

What should young people do with their lives today? Many things, obviously. But the most daring thing is to create stable communities in which the terrible disease of loneliness can be cured.

—*Kurt Vonnegut*

CONNECTION

My favorite things in life don't cost any money. It's really clear that the most precious resource we all have is time.

—*Steve Jobs*

Whether you think you can or
you think you can't, you're right.

—Henry Ford

SELF-AFFIRMATION

PURPOSE

If a man is called to be a street sweeper, he should sweep streets even as a Michelangelo painted, or Beethoven composed music or Shakespeare wrote poetry. He should sweep streets so well that all the hosts of heaven and earth will pause to say, "Here lived a great street sweeper who did his job well."

—*Martin Luther King Jr.*

DAY 234

A morning-glory at my window satisfies
me more than the metaphysics of books.

—*Walt Whitman, "Song of Myself"*

Whatever you can do, or dream you can, begin it.
Boldness has genius, power, and magic in it.

—*Johann Wolfgang von Goethe, translated by John Anster*

INTENTION

For after all, the best thing one
can do
When it is raining, is let it rain.

—*Henry Wadsworth Longfellow,*
"The Birds of Killingworth"

CALM

Have a heart that never hardens, and a temper that never tires, and a touch that never hurts.

—*Charles Dickens*, Our Mutual Friend

CONNECTION

A sensible man takes pleasure
in what he has instead of
pining for what he has not.

—*Democritus*

GRATITUDE

I am an expression of the divine,
just like a peach is, just like a fish is.
I have a right to be this way. . . . We
will never have to be other than who
we are in order to be successful. . . .
We realize that we are as ourselves
unlimited and our experiences valid.

—*Alice Walker*, The Color Purple

SELF-AFFIRMATION

A man can be as great as he wants to be. If you believe in yourself and have the courage, the determination, the dedication, the competitive drive and if you are willing to sacrifice the little things in life and pay the price for the things that are worthwhile, it can be done.

—*Vince Lombardi*

PURPOSE

Breathe. Let go. And remind yourself that this very moment is the only one you know you have for sure. —*Oprah Winfrey*

PRESENCE

DAY 242

Life shrinks or expands in
proportion to one's courage.

—*Anaïs Nin*

INTENTION

CALM

True life is lived when
tiny changes occur.

—*Leo Tolstoy*

Honey itself cannot vie with well-framed words, for heart's comfort and body's refreshment.

—*Proverbs 16:24*

CONNECTION

DAY 245

With the new day comes new strength and new thoughts.

—*Eleanor Roosevelt*

GRATITUDE

I don't know if our life has a purpose and I don't see that it matters. What does matter is that we're a part. Like a thread in a cloth or a grass-blade in a field. It *is* and we *are*.

—*Ursula K. Le Guin,* The Lathe of Heaven

When the whole world
is silent, even one voice
becomes powerful.

—*Malala Yousafzai*

PURPOSE

It takes two to
speak the truth—
one to speak, and
another to hear.

—*Henry David Thoreau*

PRESENCE

INTENTION

DAY 249

The only person you are
destined to become is the
person you decide to be.

—*Ralph Waldo Emerson*

The darker the night,
the brighter the stars.

—*Fyodor Dostoyevsky,*
Crime and Punishment

CALM

DAY 251

A wonderful fact to reflect upon, that every human creature is constituted to be that profound secret and mystery to every other. —*Charles Dickens*, A Tale of Two Cities

Happiness does not depend
on outward things but on
the way we see them.

—*Leo Tolstoy*

GRATITUDE

DAY 253

When we are not sure, we are alive.

—*Graham Greene*

If you're bored with life—you don't get
up every morning with a burning desire to
do things—you don't have enough goals.

—Lou Holtz

PURPOSE

Many people lose the small joys in the hope for the big happiness.

—*Pearl S. Buck*

PRESENCE

The future belongs
to those who believe
in the beauty of
their dreams.

—*Eleanor Roosevelt*

INTENTION

Strange as it may seem, I still hope
for the best, even though the best,
like an interesting piece of mail,
so rarely arrives, and even when it
does it can be lost so easily.

—*Lemony Snicket,* The Beatrice Letters

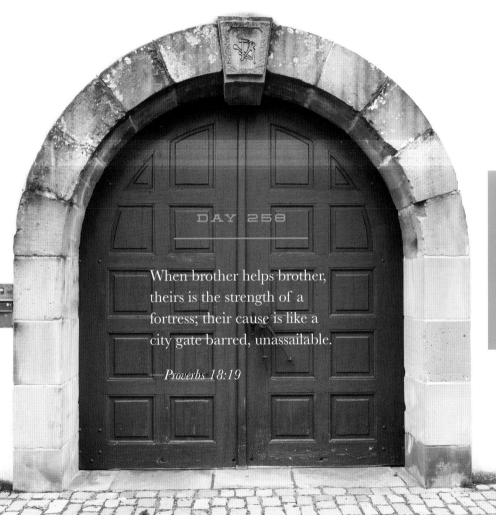

DAY 258

When brother helps brother,
theirs is the strength of a
fortress; their cause is like a
city gate barred, unassailable.

—*Proverbs 18:19*

GRATITUDE

[Gratitude] is not only
the greatest of virtues but
the parent of all others.

—*Cicero*

The lesson I've learned the most often in life is that you're always going to know more in the future than you know now.

—*Taylor Swift*

PURPOSE

If you want to resolve a dispute or come out from conflict, the very first thing is to speak the truth. If you have a headache and tell the doctor you have a stomachache, how can the doctor help? You must speak the truth. The truth will abolish fear.

—*Ziauddin Yousafzai, as quoted by Malala Yousafzai,* I Am Malala

I cannot teach anybody
anything. I can only
make them think.

—*Socrates*

PRESENCE

Discipline is the soul of an army. It makes
small numbers formidable; procures success
to the weak and esteem to all.

—*George Washington*

INTENTION

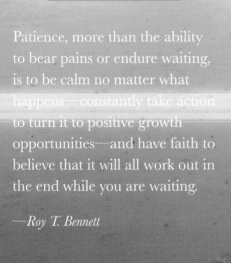

Patience, more than the ability
to bear pains or endure waiting,
is to be calm no matter what
happens—constantly take action
to turn it to positive growth
opportunities—and have faith to
believe that it will all work out in
the end while you are waiting.

—*Roy T. Bennett*

CALM

No one is useless in this world . . .
who lightens the burdens of it for
anyone else.

—*Charles Dickens,* Our Mutual Friend

CONNECTION

Appreciation
is a wonderful
thing. It makes
what is excellent
in others belong
to us as well.

—*Voltaire*

GRATITUDE

You're braver than you believe, and stronger than you seem, and smarter than you think.

—*Christopher Robin*, Pooh's Grand Adventure: The Search for Christopher Robin

SELF-AFFIRMATION

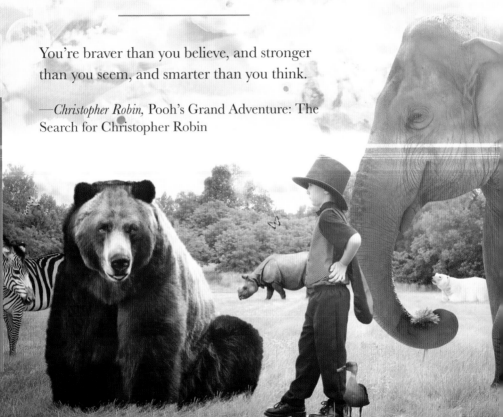

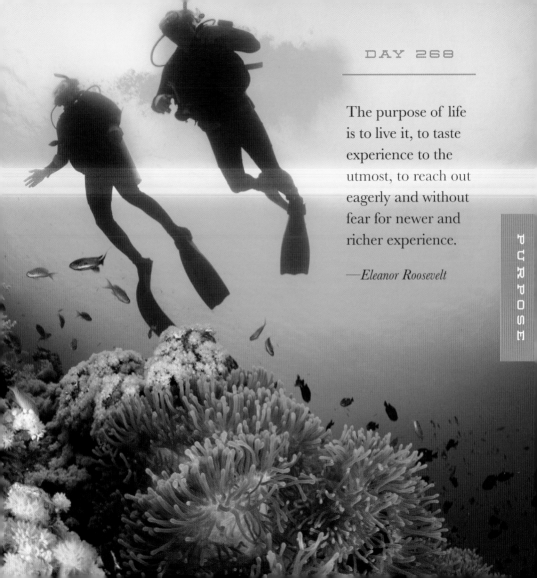

The purpose of life
is to live it, to taste
experience to the
utmost, to reach out
eagerly and without
fear for newer and
richer experience.

—*Eleanor Roosevelt*

PURPOSE

I believe a leaf of grass is no less than the journey work of the stars,
And the pismire is equally perfect, and a grain of sand, and the egg
of the wren.

—*Walt Whitman, "Song of Myself"*

PRESENCE

You may have to fight a battle
more than once to win it.

—*Margaret Thatcher*

INTENTION

All human wisdom is contained in these two words—wait and hope.

—*Alexandre Dumas*, The Count of Monte Cristo

CALM

To serve is beautiful, but only if it is done
with joy and a whole heart and a free mind.

—*Pearl S. Buck*

My parents are the coolest of the cool on every single level, and it's because they have a deep appreciation for every moment of their lives.

—*Rashida Jones*

GRATITUDE

Accepting oneself does not preclude an attempt to become better.

—*Flannery O'Connor*, The Habit of Being

SELF-AFFIRMATION

PURPOSE

If you want to identify me, ask me not where I live, or what I like to eat, or how I comb my hair, but ask me what I am living for, in detail; ask me what I think is keeping me from living fully for the thing I want to live for.

—*Thomas Merton*

Stop a moment, cease your work, look around you.

—*Leo Tolstoy*, Essays, Letters, and Miscellanies

PRESENCE

The end of a melody
is not its goal: but
nonetheless, had the
melody not reached its
end it would not have
reached its goal either.

—*Friedrich Nietzsche*,
The Wanderer and
His Shadow

INTENTION

If you want to
be happy, be so.

—*Kozma Prutkov*

CALM

DAY 279

I believe that every single event
in life happens in an opportunity
to choose love over fear.

—*Oprah Winfrey*

Gratitude and attitude are not
challenges; they are choices.

—*Robert Braathe*

I have been bent and
broken, but—I hope—
into a better shape.

—*Charles Dickens,*
Great Expectations

SELF-AFFIRMATION

To begin is easy; to persevere is
sanctity. Let your perseverance
not be a blind consequence
of the first impulse, the work
of inertia: let it be a reflective
perseverance.

—*Saint Josemaría Escrivá*, The Way

PURPOSE

PRESENCE

Keep good
company, read
good books, love
good things, and
cultivate soul and
body as faithfully
as you can.

—*Louisa May Alcott*,
Rose in Bloom

Do not stop thinking of life as an adventure. You have no security unless you can live bravely, excitingly, imaginatively; unless you can choose a challenge instead of competence.

—*Eleanor Roosevelt*

INTENTION

CALM

DAY 285

Faith is taking the first step even when
you can't see the whole staircase.

—*Martin Luther King Jr.*

One word or a pleasing
smile is often enough
to raise up a saddened
and wounded soul.

—*Saint Thérèse of Lisieux*

CONNECTION

In normal life we hardly realize how much more we receive than we give, and life cannot be rich without such gratitude. It is so easy to overestimate the importance of our own achievements compared with what we owe to the help of others.

—*Deitrich Bonhoeffer,*
Letters and Papers from Prison

GRATITUDE

Giving up doesn't
always mean you're
weak; sometimes
you're just strong
enough to let go.

—*Unknown*

SELF-AFFIRMATION

PURPOSE

The great thing in this world is not so much where we stand as in what direction we are moving.

—*Oliver Wendell Holmes Sr.*, The Autocrat of the Breakfast Table

Grown-up people do not know
that a child can give exceedingly
good advice even in the most
difficult case.

—*Fyodor Dostoyevsky,*
The Idiot

PRESENCE

If you don't behave as you believe, you
will end by believing as you behave.

—*Archbishop Fulton J. Sheen*

INTENTION

If you look for perfection,
you'll never be content.

—*Leo Tolstoy*, Anna Karenina

For we are made for co-operation, like feet, like hands, like eyelids, like the rows of the upper and lower teeth. To act against one another then is contrary to nature; and it is acting against one another to be vexed and to turn away.

—*Marcus Aurelius*, Meditations, Book 2

CONNECTION

Procrastination is the thief of time. Collar him!

—*Charles Dickens,*
David Copperfield

PURPOSE

Your beliefs will be
the light by which
you see, but they will
not be what you see
and they will not be a
substitute for seeing.

—*Flannery O'Connor,*
Mystery and Manners

PRESENCE

DAY 298

Truth will ultimately prevail
where there [are] pains
taken to bring it to light.

—*George Washington*

We must accept finite
disappointment but
never lose infinite hope.

—*Martin Luther King Jr.*

DAY 300

The more you are motivated
by love, the more fearless
and free your action will be.

—*Dalai Lama XIV*

DAY 301

The unthankful heart
discovers no mercies; but
the thankful heart will
find, in every hour, some
heavenly blessings.

—*Henry Ward Beecher*

Because one believes in oneself, one doesn't try to convince others. Because one is content with oneself, one doesn't need others' approval. Because one accepts oneself, the whole world accepts him or her.

—*Lao Tzu*

SELF-AFFIRMATION

True glory consists in doing
what deserves to be written,
in writing what deserves to
be read, and in so living as to
make the world happier and
better for our living in it.

—*Pliny the Elder*

PURPOSE

Be here now.

—*Ram Dass,* Be Here Now

A mind well schooled sees the way of life stretching upwards, leading away from the pit beneath.

—*Proverbs 15:24*

INTENTION

Smile, breathe, and
go slowly.

—*Thich Nhat Hanh*

CALM

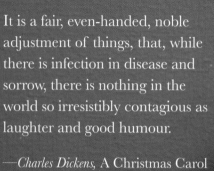

It is a fair, even-handed, noble adjustment of things, that, while there is infection in disease and sorrow, there is nothing in the world so irresistibly contagious as laughter and good humour.

—*Charles Dickens*, A Christmas Carol

CONNECTION

Not what we say about our
blessings, but how we use
them, is the true measure
of our thanksgiving.

—*W. T. Purkiser*

GRATITUDE

SELF-AFFIRMATION

DAY 309

The most common way
people give up their
power is by thinking
they don't have any.

—*Alice Walker*

DAY 310

Be a lamp, or a lifeboat, or a ladder.
Help someone's soul heal.
Walk out of your house like a shepherd.

—*Rumi*, Diwan-e Shams-e Tabrizi

PURPOSE

Don't tell me the moon is shining; show me the glint of light on broken glass.

—*Unknown*

PRESENCE

Happiness is not a goal . . . it's
a by-product of a life well lived.

—*Eleanor Roosevelt*

INTENTION

CALM

DAY 313

You can't always control
what goes on outside. But
you can always control
what goes on inside.

—*Wayne Dyer*

Kind hearts are the gardens,
Kind thoughts are the roots,
Kind words are the flowers,
Kind deeds are the fruits.
Take care of your garden
And keep out the weeds,
Fill it with sunshine,
Kind words,
And kind deeds.

—*Henry Wadsworth Longfellow*

CONNECTION

DAY 315

Never in the field of human
conflict was so much owed
by so many to so few.

—*Winston Churchill*

You may not always have a comfortable life.
And you will not always be able to solve all of
the world's problems at once. But don't ever
underestimate the importance you can have,
because history has shown us that courage can be
contagious and hope can take on a life of its own.

—*Michelle Obama*

SELF-AFFIRMATION

Make your work to be in
keeping with your purpose.

—*Leonardo da Vinci*

PURPOSE

DAY 318

Don't underestimate the value of Doing
Nothing, of just going along, listening to all
the things you can't hear, and not bothering.

—*Piglet*, Pooh's Little Instruction Book

All our dreams can
come true if we have the
courage to pursue them.

—*Walt Disney*

INTENTION

Calmness is the cradle of power.

—*J. G. Holland*

CALM

Love is our true destiny. We do not find the meaning
of life by ourselves alone—we find it with another.

—*Thomas Merton,* Love and Living

CONNECTION

Everything has beauty,
but not everyone sees it.

—*Confucius*

GRATITUDE

DAY 323

No one can make
you feel inferior
without your consent.

—Eleanor Roosevelt

Every man is said to have his peculiar ambition. Whether it be true or not, I can say for one that I have no other so great as that of being truly esteemed of my fellow men, by rendering myself worthy of their esteem.

—*Abraham Lincoln*

PURPOSE

Time can't be measured in days
the way money is measured in
pesos and *centavos*, because all
pesos are equal, while every day,
perhaps every hour, is different.

—*Jorge Luis Borges*

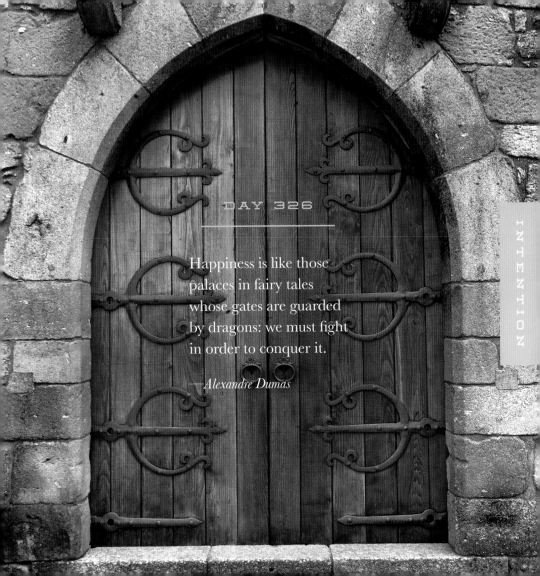

DAY 326

Happiness is like those palaces in fairy tales whose gates are guarded by dragons: we must fight in order to conquer it.

—*Alexandre Dumas*

INTENTION

The only true wisdom is in
knowing you know nothing.

—*Socrates*

There are two ways of
spreading light: to be the candle
or the mirror that reflects it.

—*Edith Wharton*

CONNECTION

DAY 329

What separates privilege
from entitlement is gratitude.

—*Brené Brown*

DAY 930

I don't have to prove anything to anyone. I only have to follow my heart and concentrate on what I want to say to the world. I run my world. —*Beyoncé*

SELF-AFFIRMATION

PURPOSE

DAY 331

If more of us valued food
and cheer and song above
hoarded gold, it would be
a merrier world.

—*J. R. R. Tolkien*, The Hobbit

My life has been the poem I would have writ,
But I could not both live and utter it.

—*Henry David Thoreau, "My Life Has Been the Poem"*

PRESENCE

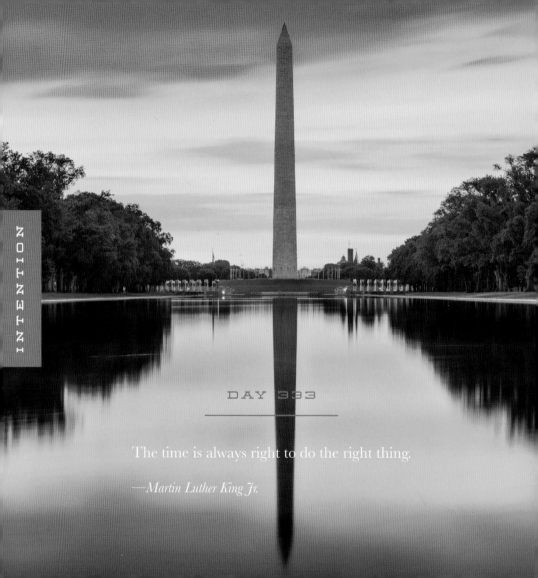

INTENTION

DAY 333

The time is always right to do the right thing.

—*Martin Luther King Jr.*

If people just took it
a day at a time, they'd
be a lot happier.

—*Stephen King*,
The Long Walk

CALM

Be kind whenever
possible. It is
always possible.

—*Dalai Lama XIV*

CONNECTION

Feeling gratitude and not expressing it is
like wrapping a present and not giving it.

—*William Arthur Ward*

GRATITUDE

DAY 337

Be faithful in small things,
because it is in them that
your strength lies.

—*Unknown*

DAY 338

Always bear in mind that your own resolution to succeed is more important than any other one thing.

—*Abraham Lincoln*

That which we call a rose
By any other name would smell as sweet.

—*William Shakespeare*, Romeo and Juliet

PRESENCE

Everyone thinks of changing
the world, but no one thinks
of changing himself.

—*Leo Tolstoy*

INTENTION

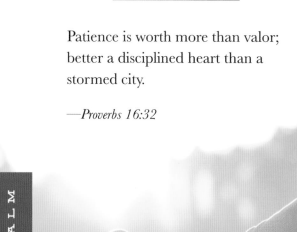

Patience is worth more than valor; better a disciplined heart than a stormed city.

—*Proverbs 16:32*

CALM

There is no happiness like that of being loved by your fellow-creatures, and feeling that your presence is an addition to their comfort.

—*Charlotte Brontë*, Jane Eyre

CONNECTION

GRATITUDE

DAY 343

If you want to turn
your life around, try
thankfulness. It will
change your life mightily.

—*Gerald Good*

We delight in the beauty
of the butterfly but rarely
admit the changes it has
gone through to achieve
that beauty.

—*Maya Angelou*

SELF-AFFIRMATION

DAY 345

—————————

Man know thyself;
then thou shalt know
the Universe and God.

—*Pythagoras*

DAY 346

I have never let
my schooling
interfere with
my education.

—*Unknown*

PRESENCE

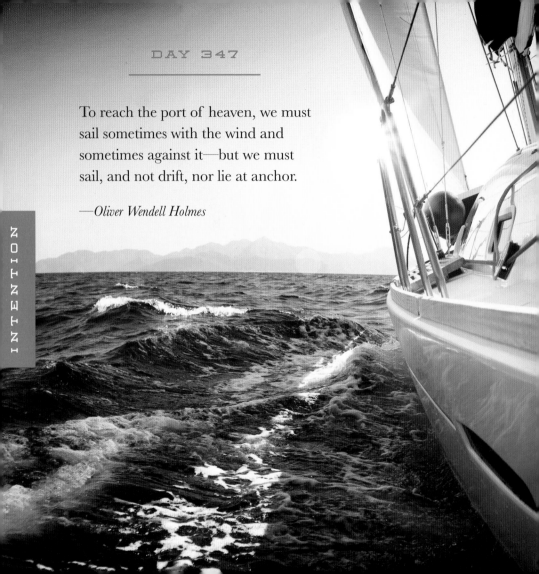

To reach the port of heaven, we must sail sometimes with the wind and sometimes against it—but we must sail, and not drift, nor lie at anchor.

—*Oliver Wendell Holmes*

INTENTION

Angels can fly
because they can take
themselves lightly.

—*G. K. Chesterton*

CALM

DAY 349

Darkness cannot drive out darkness: only light can do that. Hate cannot drive out hate: only love can do that.

—*Martin Luther King Jr.*

"Thank you" is a wonderful phrase. Use it. It will add stature to your soul.

—*Marjorie Pay Hinckley,* Small and Simple Things

GRATITUDE

SELF-AFFIRMATION

You probably . . . wouldn't worry about what people think of you if you could know how seldom they do!

—*Olin Miller*

Always do what is right. It
will gratify half of mankind
and astound the other.

—*Mark Twain*

PURPOSE

Fortune sides with
him who dares.

—*Virgil*

PRESENCE

It is not enough to be industrious; so are the ants.
What are you industrious about? —*Henry David Thoreau*

INTENTION

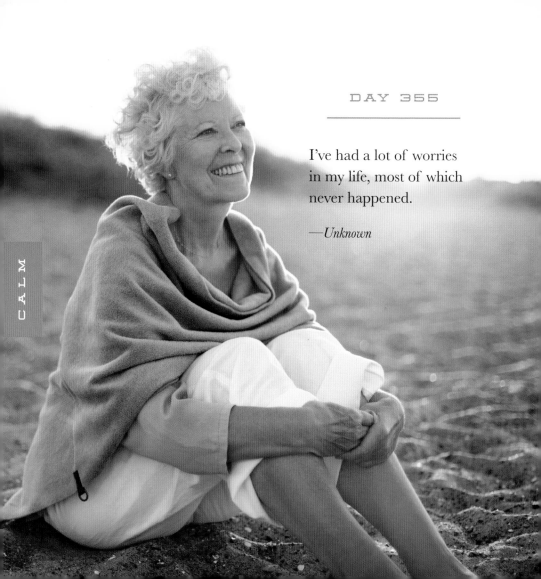

CALM

I've had a lot of worries
in my life, most of which
never happened.

—*Unknown*

What you leave behind is not what is engraved in stone monuments but what is woven into the lives of others.

—*Pericles*

CONNECTION

Oh blessed perseverance of the donkey that turns the water-wheel! Always the same pace. Always the same circles. One day after another: every day the same. Without that, there would be no ripeness in the fruit, nor blossom in the orchard, nor scent of flowers in the garden.

—*Saint Josemaría Escrivá*, The Way

GRATITUDE

I'm proud of myself for doing my best. That's all anyone can ask of me.

—*Stefanie Weisman*, The Secrets of Top Students

SELF-AFFIRMATION

PURPOSE

I've come to
believe that
each of us has a
personal calling
that's as unique as
a fingerprint—and
that the best way
to succeed is to
discover what you
love and then find
a way to offer it to
others in the form
of service, working
hard, and also
allowing the energy
of the universe to
lead you.

—*Oprah Winfrey*

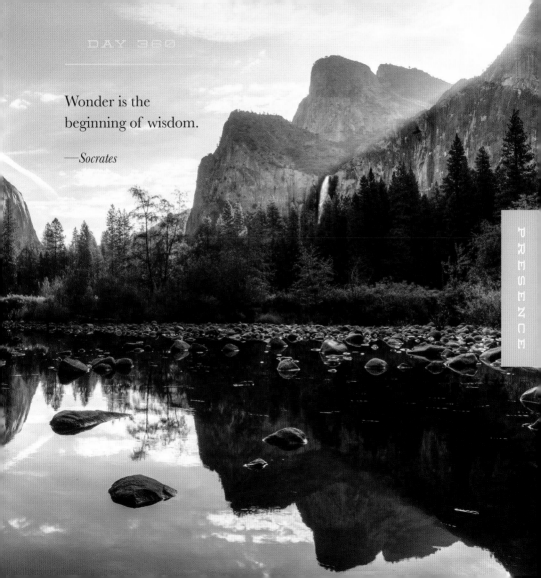

Wonder is the
beginning of wisdom.

—*Socrates*

PRESENCE

It does not matter how slowly
you go as long as you do not stop.

—*Confucius*

INTENTION

Nothing is so aggravating as calmness.

—*Mahatma Gandhi*

CALM

To forgive is the highest, most beautiful form of love. In return, you will receive untold peace and happiness.

—*Robert Muller*

CONNECTION

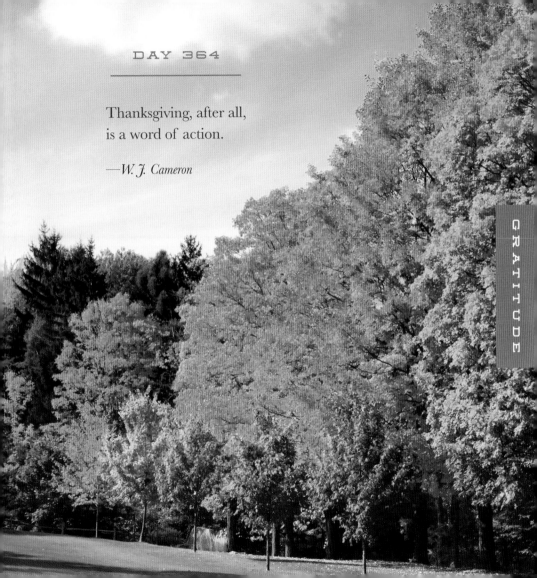

Thanksgiving, after all,
is a word of action.

—*W. J. Cameron*

GRATITUDE

SELF-AFFIRMATION

DAY 365

It is never too late to be
what you might have been.

—*Unknown*

ABOUT FAMILIUS

Welcome to a place where mothers and fathers are celebrated, not belittled. Where values are at the core of happy family life. Where boo-boos are still kissed, cake beaters are still licked, and mistakes are still okay. Welcome to a place where books—and family—are beautiful. Familius: a book publisher dedicated to helping families be happy.

If you feel a few friends and family might benefit from what you've read, let us know and we'll be happy to provide you with quantity discounts. Simply email us at specialorders@familius.com.

Website: www.familius.com
Facebook: www.facebook.com/paterfamilius
Twitter: @familiustalk, @paterfamilius1
Pinterest: www.pinterest.com/familius
Instagram: @familiustalk

The most important work you ever do will be within the walls of your own home.

FAMILIUS

Published by Familius LLC, www.familius.com

Familius books are available at special discounts for bulk purchases, whether for sales promotions or for family or corporate use. For more information, contact Familius Sales at 559-876-2170 or email orders@familius.com.

Library of Congress Cataloging-in-Publication Data
2016962609   ISBN 9781944822545

Quotes compiled by Elena Gonzalez
Edited by Sarah Echard
Cover and book design by David Miles
Photography credits: Shutterstock.com

Printed in China

10 9 8 7 6 5 4 3

First Edition